Mastering

FIBONACCI RETRACEMENT

.

in Trading

A Comprehensive Guide

by

Lalit Mohanty

PREFACE

Welcome to the fascinating world of Fibonacci analysis in financial markets. As the financial landscape continues to evolve, traders and investors seek reliable tools to navigate the complexities of price movements and trends. Among the various methods available, Fibonacci analysis stands out for its mathematical elegance and practical applications.

This guide is designed to be a comprehensive resource for individuals looking to explore, understand, and master the art of Fibonacci analysis in trading. Whether you're a seasoned trader seeking to enhance your technical analysis toolkit or a newcomer eager to grasp the fundamentals, this guide aims to provide valuable insights, practical strategies, and a roadmap for continuous learning.

The journey begins with an introduction to the history and origin of Fibonacci analysis, delving into the mathematical intricacies of the Fibonacci sequence and the golden ratio. From there, we progress to understanding market trends, exploring Fibonacci retracement levels, and selecting appropriate tools and platforms for effective analysis. The guide unfolds through practical applications, real-life examples, and considerations for developing a systematic trading strategy.

Chapters on advanced techniques, pitfalls, and challenges provide a well-rounded perspective, preparing you for the intricacies of applying Fibonacci analysis in dynamic market conditions. The integration of technology and automation, along with case studies and success stories, illustrates the real-world impact of Fibonacci in trading.

As we delve into the psychological aspects of Fibonacci trading, exploring topics such as building confidence, overcoming anxiety, and fostering patience and discipline, the guide emphasizes the importance of a holistic approach to trading. Mastering Fibonacci analysis requires not only technical proficiency but also a resilient mindset and continuous learning.

The latter part of the guide ventures into the future of Fibonacci in financial markets, considering emerging trends, potential developments, and the intersection of Fibonacci analysis with sustainability and ethical trading practices. The appendix serves as a valuable resource, offering recommended books, online courses, trading software, a glossary, and key terms to support your ongoing education and application of Fibonacci techniques.

Embark on this journey with an open mind and a commitment to lifelong learning. Whether you're a trader, investor, or enthusiast, may this guide serve as a compass in your exploration of Fibonacci analysis, empowering you to make informed decisions and navigate the ever-changing landscape of financial markets.

Lalit Mohanty

Table of Contents

Appendix: Fibonacci Resources and Tools

Recommended Books

Online Courses

Trading Software and Tools

Glossary

Key Terms and Concepts

CHAPTER 1

INTRODUCTION TO FIBONACCI RETRACEMENT

1.1 What is Fibonacci Retracement?

In the intricate tapestry of financial markets, traders often seek tools that can decipher the complexities of price movements and aid in making informed decisions. One such tool that has stood the test of time is Fibonacci retracement. At its essence, Fibonacci retracement is a technical analysis method employed to identify potential reversal levels within a financial asset's price trend.

The concept hinges on the notion that after a significant price movement—whether upward or downward—retracement levels can be predicted using ratios derived from the Fibonacci sequence. By applying these ratios to key price points, traders can anticipate where a trend might pause, correct, or even reverse. The ability of Fibonacci retracement to provide a systematic approach to understanding market behavior makes it a valuable asset in the trader's toolkit.

1.2 History and Origin

To truly appreciate the power of Fibonacci retracement, one must delve into its historical roots. The origins can be traced back to the 13th century and the work of an Italian mathematician named Leonardo Fibonacci. While he is most renowned for introducing the Fibonacci sequence to the Western world, it was not until much later that traders recognized the sequence's relevance in financial markets.

Fibonacci's Liber Abaci, published in 1202, introduced the sequence as a solution to a mathematical problem involving rabbit breeding. Little did Fibonacci know that his sequence, where each number is the sum of the two preceding ones (0, 1, 1, 2, 3, 5, 8, 13, and so on), would become a cornerstone of technical analysis in the realm of trading.

1.3 The Fibonacci Sequence

The Fibonacci sequence, often dubbed nature's numbering system, manifests itself in various natural phenomena, from the spirals of seashells to the arrangement of leaves on a stem. In the context of trading, this sequence holds the key to identifying potential retracement levels.

As traders apply the Fibonacci ratios derived from this sequence—such as the golden ratio (1.618) and its inverse (0.618)—to significant price highs and lows, a set of retracement levels emerges. These levels, expressed as percentages, become invaluable guides for traders seeking potential support or resistance areas within a given trend.

1.4 The Golden Ratio

At the heart of Fibonacci retracement lies the golden ratio, a mathematical constant approximately equal to 1.618. Often denoted by the Greek letter Phi (Φ), this ratio plays a pivotal role in the determination of retracement levels. The golden ratio's aesthetic significance in art, architecture, and nature further underscores its relevance in financial markets.

Understanding how the golden ratio influences price movements empowers traders to anticipate key reversal points with a heightened level of precision. As we explore Fibonacci retracement further, the golden ratio will emerge as a guiding principle, shaping our approach to market analysis.

1.5 Application in Financial Markets

The practical application of Fibonacci retracement in financial markets spans a multitude of assets, including stocks, currencies, commodities, and cryptocurrencies. Traders utilize this tool to identify potential entry and exit points, set stop-loss orders, and determine the optimal placement of take-profit levels.

By integrating Fibonacci retracement into their technical analysis arsenal, traders aim to navigate the intricate dance of market trends with increased confidence and precision. As we journey through the subsequent chapters, we will unravel the intricacies of applying Fibonacci retracement in real-world trading scenarios, equipping you with the knowledge to master this powerful tool in your pursuit of trading success.

CHAPTER 2

UNDERSTANDING MARKET TRENDS

2.1 Basics of Market Trends

Before delving into the intricacies of Fibonacci retracement, it is imperative to establish a solid foundation in understanding market trends. Trends form the bedrock of technical analysis, providing traders with valuable insights into the direction and momentum of an asset's price movement.

In essence, a market trend reflects the general direction in which prices are moving. Recognizing and comprehending these trends are crucial for traders aiming to make informed decisions. Understanding the basics involves identifying three primary types of trends:

- **Uptrend:** Characterized by higher highs and higher lows, an uptrend indicates a bullish market sentiment where buyers dominate.

- **Downtrend:** Marked by lower highs and lower lows, a downtrend signals a bearish market sentiment with sellers in control.

- **Sideways or Range-bound Trend:** When prices move within a horizontal range, lacking a clear upward or downward bias, the market is considered to be in a sideways or range-bound trend.

2.2 Identifying Bullish and Bearish Trends

The ability to identify bullish and bearish trends is a foundational skill for traders. Various technical indicators and chart patterns aid in this identification process. Moving averages, trendlines, and price patterns contribute to the analysis, providing visual cues that help discern the prevailing market sentiment.

Bullish trends are often accompanied by strong buying activity, resulting in upward price movements. Conversely, bearish trends are characterized by increased selling pressure, leading to a downward trajectory in prices. Traders keen on mastering Fibonacci retracement must first become adept at recognizing and interpreting these fundamental trends.

2.3 The Role of Fibonacci in Trend Analysis

Fibonacci retracement finds its niche in trend analysis by offering a systematic method for identifying potential reversal levels within an ongoing trend. As prices move in a particular direction, traders can apply Fibonacci ratios to pinpoint levels where a retracement or reversal might occur.

By aligning Fibonacci retracement levels with key highs and lows in a trend, traders gain valuable insights into potential support and resistance zones. This aids in decision-making, allowing for strategic entry and exit points that align with the broader market trend.

2.4 Fibonacci as a Tool for Trend Confirmation

In addition to identifying potential reversal points, Fibonacci retracement serves as a powerful tool for confirming existing trends. When retracement levels align with established support or resistance areas, the likelihood of a trend continuation is reinforced.

Traders often observe how price reacts to Fibonacci levels in conjunction with other technical indicators. Confirming the alignment of Fibonacci retracement with trendlines, moving averages, or chart patterns enhances the reliability of trend analysis.

As we progress through this guide, we will explore practical examples of using Fibonacci retracement to confirm and enhance trend analysis, providing you with a comprehensive understanding of how this tool seamlessly integrates into the broader framework of technical analysis.

CHAPTER 3

FIBONACCI RETRACEMENT LEVELS

3.1 Key Fibonacci Levels

Central to the application of Fibonacci retracement in trading are the key levels derived from the Fibonacci sequence. These levels, expressed as percentages, play a pivotal role in identifying potential retracement zones within a price trend. The primary Fibonacci retracement levels include:

- **23.6% Retracement Level:** This level represents the first significant Fibonacci retracement, suggesting a shallow pullback in the price. Traders often view this level as an initial area of interest for potential reversals.

- **38.2% Retracement Level:** Considered one of the most crucial levels, the 38.2% retracement often acts as a strong support or resistance zone. Traders frequently use this level to gauge the depth of a retracement within a trend.

- **50% Retracement Level:** While not a Fibonacci ratio per se, the 50% level is widely used in technical analysis. Some traders consider this level as a potential reversal point, while others see it as a zone of indecision.

- **61.8% Retracement Level (Golden Ratio):** Revered for its significance in Fibonacci analysis, the 61.8% level is often referred to as the golden ratio. This level frequently marks a key support or resistance area and is closely watched by traders for potential trend reversals.

- **78.6% Retracement Level:** Though not as commonly used as the previous levels, the 78.6% retracement can be relevant in certain market conditions. Traders may consider this level as an extended retracement, signaling a deeper pullback in the price.

3.2 0.382 Retracement Level

The 0.382 retracement level, derived from the inverse of the golden ratio, is a key Fibonacci level indicating a moderate retracement within a trend. Traders often observe how price reacts around this level to gauge the strength of the prevailing trend. If the price bounces off the 0.382 level, it may signal a robust continuation of the trend.

Understanding the significance of the 0.382 retracement level is crucial for traders seeking optimal entry points. This level serves as a guide for setting stop-loss orders and helps in determining the risk-reward ratio for a given trade.

3.3 0.500 Retracement Level

The 0.500 retracement level, although not a traditional Fibonacci ratio, is widely recognized in technical analysis. Positioned at the midpoint between the high and low of a price movement, the 50% level is often perceived as a zone of equilibrium. Traders interpret price behavior around this level to assess whether the prevailing trend will persist or if a reversal is imminent.

The 0.500 retracement level is particularly relevant in markets exhibiting a strong directional bias. If the price holds above this level during a retracement, it may indicate the resilience of the prevailing trend.

3.4 0.618 Retracement Level

Often referred to as the golden ratio, the 0.618 retracement level is a key focal point for traders employing Fibonacci analysis. This level frequently serves as a robust support or resistance zone, influencing trading decisions in both bullish and bearish markets.

When the price approaches the 0.618 retracement level, traders closely monitor price action for signs of a reversal or continuation. The golden ratio's prevalence in natural phenomena, coupled with its consistent influence on price movements, underscores its significance in technical analysis.

3.5 Additional Levels and Extensions

Beyond the core Fibonacci retracement levels, traders may also explore additional levels and extensions to refine their analysis. Common extensions include the 1.618, 2.618, and 4.236 levels, which signify potential areas of trend continuation after a retracement. These extensions provide traders with a more nuanced understanding of the potential trajectory of a trend.

Integrating these extended levels into Fibonacci analysis requires a keen understanding of market conditions and the context of the price movement. While not as universally applied as the core levels, extensions can offer valuable insights for traders seeking a comprehensive view of potential price targets.

3.6 Selecting Appropriate Levels for Analysis

The selection of appropriate Fibonacci levels for analysis depends on various factors, including the timeframe of the chart, the volatility of the asset, and the trader's risk tolerance. Short-term traders may focus on shallower retracement levels, such as 23.6% and 38.2%, for quick trades, while long-term investors may pay more attention to deeper retracement levels for strategic entry points.

Additionally, combining Fibonacci levels with other technical indicators and chart patterns enhances the precision of analysis. The art of selecting appropriate levels involves considering the broader market context and using Fibonacci retracement as a complementary tool within a comprehensive trading strategy.

As we progress through this guide, we will delve deeper into practical examples and case studies, illustrating how to effectively apply Fibonacci retracement levels in real-world trading scenarios. Understanding the nuances of each level and their interplay in different market conditions will empower you to make informed and strategic trading decisions.

CHAPTER 4

FIBONACCI RETRACEMENT TOOLS AND PLATFORMS

4.1 Popular Trading Platforms

In the ever-evolving landscape of online trading, a plethora of platforms cater to the diverse needs of traders. Choosing the right platform is crucial for seamless integration of Fibonacci retracement into your technical analysis toolkit. Here, we explore some popular trading platforms that offer robust tools for Fibonacci analysis:

- **MetaTrader 4 (MT4):** Renowned for its user-friendly interface and extensive charting capabilities, MT4 is a staple for many traders. It provides built-in Fibonacci retracement tools and allows users to draw retracement levels effortlessly.

- **MetaTrader 5 (MT5):** An upgraded version of MT4, MT5 offers additional features, including more timeframes, economic calendar integration, and improved charting tools. Fibonacci retracement is seamlessly integrated into the charting package, enhancing the analytical capabilities of traders.

- **Thinkorswim:** TD Ameritrade's Thinkorswim platform is a sophisticated option for traders seeking in-depth analysis tools. With a customizable interface, advanced charting, and a comprehensive set of technical indicators, Thinkorswim allows for seamless application of Fibonacci retracement.

- **TradingView:** A web-based platform known for its social trading features and advanced charting tools, TradingView is widely used by traders and investors. Its intuitive interface allows users to apply Fibonacci retracement easily, and the platform supports customization for personalized analysis.

- **NinjaTrader:** Ideal for both beginners and advanced traders, NinjaTrader offers a range of tools for technical analysis. Traders can apply Fibonacci retracement with precision, and the platform's flexibility allows for customization based on individual preferences.

4.2 Fibonacci Tools on Trading Platforms

Understanding how to leverage Fibonacci tools on popular trading platforms is essential for effective analysis. These platforms typically provide the following Fibonacci tools:

- **Fibonacci Retracement Tool:** The core tool for applying Fibonacci retracement levels to price charts. Traders can select the tool, identify the swing high and low points, and the platform automatically draws the retracement levels.

- **Fibonacci Expansion Tool:** Extending the analysis beyond retracement levels, the expansion tool helps identify potential price targets during trend continuation. Traders can project extension levels to anticipate where a trend might unfold.

- **Fibonacci Time Zones:** Some platforms offer Fibonacci time zone tools, allowing traders to analyze the duration of price movements. These time zones can help identify potential turning points in the market based on time cycles.

- **Fibonacci Fans and Arcs:** Advanced tools like Fibonacci fans and arcs provide additional insights into potential support and resistance areas. These tools complement retracement analysis by offering a broader perspective on price movements.

4.3 Customizing Fibonacci Settings

While trading platforms come with default Fibonacci settings, customizing these settings can enhance the precision of your analysis. Key customization options include:

- **Color and Line Style:** Traders can choose colors and line styles for different Fibonacci levels, making it easier to differentiate between retracement levels on the chart.

- **Level Values:** Some platforms allow users to display or hide the numerical values of Fibonacci levels on the chart. Customizing the display of these values can streamline the analysis process.

- **Default Ratios:** Customizing default ratios enables traders to set preferred Fibonacci levels for quicker analysis. This is particularly useful for those who have specific ratios that align with their trading strategy.

- **Timeframe Preferences:** Adjusting the default timeframe settings for Fibonacci tools allows traders to apply the analysis across different timeframes, catering to various trading styles.

4.4 Drawing Accurate Retracement Lines

Drawing accurate retracement lines is a fundamental skill for effective Fibonacci analysis. The process involves:

- **Selecting Swing High and Low Points:** Identifying the correct swing high and low points is crucial. These points anchor the Fibonacci retracement tool, determining the scope of the analysis.

- **Understanding Trend Direction:** The accuracy of retracement analysis depends on correctly identifying the prevailing trend. Whether analyzing an uptrend or downtrend, aligning the tool with the direction of the trend enhances its predictive power.

- **Adjusting for Market Conditions:** Market conditions, including volatility and the timeframe of the chart, can impact the accuracy of retracement lines. Traders should adjust the tool's sensitivity based on current market dynamics.

- **Validating with Other Indicators:** To enhance the reliability of retracement lines, traders often validate findings with other technical indicators, trendlines, or chart patterns. Consistency across multiple indicators strengthens the overall analysis.

Mastering the art of drawing accurate retracement lines requires practice and an understanding of the nuances of price action. As we progress through this guide, we will explore real-world examples, providing insights into how to navigate various market scenarios using Fibonacci retracement tools on different platforms. Armed with this knowledge, you will be equipped to harness the full potential of Fibonacci analysis in your trading endeavors.

CHAPTER 5

IDENTIFYING POTENTIAL ENTRY AND EXIT POINTS

5.1 Using Fibonacci Levels for Entry

One of the primary applications of Fibonacci retracement in trading is to identify opportune entry points. Traders leverage key Fibonacci levels to pinpoint potential reversal zones within a trend, facilitating strategic entries. Here's a breakdown of how Fibonacci levels can be employed for effective entry strategies:

- **Bounce off Key Retracement Levels:** When the price retraces to a significant Fibonacci level, such as the 38.2%, 50%, or 61.8%, traders often look for signs of a bounce. A bounce off these levels may indicate a resumption of the prevailing trend, offering an attractive entry point.

- **Confluence with Other Indicators:** Aligning Fibonacci retracement levels with other technical indicators, such as trendlines, moving averages, or support/resistance zones, strengthens the validity of an entry signal. Confluence of multiple factors enhances the likelihood of a successful trade.

- **Using Fibonacci Fans and Arcs:** Incorporating advanced Fibonacci tools like fans and arcs provides additional confirmation for entry points. These tools can highlight potential areas of support or resistance, complementing the analysis derived from retracement levels.

- **Waiting for Price Confirmation:** Rather than entering a trade immediately when the price touches a Fibonacci level, some traders prefer to wait for additional price confirmation. This may involve observing candlestick patterns, trend reversals, or other price action signals before executing a trade.

Successful entry strategies with Fibonacci retracement require a combination of technical analysis skills and a deep understanding of market dynamics. Traders should experiment with different Fibonacci levels and tools on historical charts to gain confidence in identifying optimal entry points.

5.2 Setting Stop-Loss Orders with Fibonacci

Risk management is an integral aspect of trading, and Fibonacci retracement can aid in setting effective stop-loss orders. Traders use Fibonacci levels to determine potential areas where a trend reversal might occur, establishing stop-loss orders to mitigate losses if the trade moves against them. Key considerations for setting stop-loss orders with Fibonacci include:

- **Placing Stops Beyond Key Levels:** Traders often position stop-loss orders just beyond significant Fibonacci retracement levels. This approach accounts for market noise and prevents premature exits in case of minor price fluctuations.

- **Adapting to Volatility:** In highly volatile markets, traders may adjust the distance of their stop-loss orders to accommodate larger price swings. This adaptability ensures that stops are not too tight, allowing for natural market fluctuations while still providing protection.

- **Using Fibonacci Extensions for Targets:** Some traders incorporate Fibonacci extensions to establish stop-loss targets. By projecting extension levels beyond the initial retracement, traders can identify areas where the price is likely to continue in the direction of the trend, serving as potential stop-loss points.

- **Considering Overall Risk-Reward Ratio:** Aligning stop-loss levels with the trader's risk tolerance and overall risk-reward ratio is crucial. Fibonacci retracement can be a valuable tool in optimizing risk-reward dynamics by providing logical levels for both stop-loss and take-profit orders.

Effective use of stop-loss orders with Fibonacci retracement requires a comprehensive understanding of the specific market conditions, the trader's risk appetite, and the characteristics of the asset being traded.

5.3 Take-Profit Strategies

Just as Fibonacci retracement aids in identifying entry points and setting stop-loss orders, it is equally valuable for devising take-profit strategies. Traders use Fibonacci levels to determine potential target areas where a trend might reverse or experience a significant price reaction. Key considerations for setting take-profit orders with Fibonacci include:

- **Aligning with Fibonacci Extension Levels:** Traders often use Fibonacci extension levels to identify potential price targets. Extensions beyond the initial retracement provide insights into where a trend might continue, serving as logical points for take-profit orders.

- **Assessing Confluence Zones:** When multiple Fibonacci levels, such as retracement and extension levels, converge in a specific price zone, it forms a confluence area. Traders may consider these zones as prime candidates for take-profit orders, anticipating a stronger reaction in the market.

- **Dynamic Adjustments Based on Market Conditions:** Adapting take-profit strategies to current market conditions is crucial. In trending markets, traders may allow positions to run for extended periods, while in ranging markets, shorter-term profit targets might be more appropriate.

- **Combining with Other Technical Analysis Tools:** Integrating Fibonacci retracement with other technical analysis tools, such as trendlines, support/resistance zones, or momentum indicators, enhances the reliability of take-profit strategies. Confluence of multiple signals increases the probability of achieving profit targets.

Successful take-profit strategies with Fibonacci retracement require a nuanced understanding of market dynamics and the ability to interpret price action at key levels. Traders should remain flexible and adjust their take-profit approach based on evolving market conditions.

5.4 Combining Fibonacci with Other Indicators

While Fibonacci retracement is a powerful standalone tool, combining it with other indicators enhances the precision and reliability of trading decisions. This synergy allows traders to validate signals, confirm trends, and refine entry and exit points. Here's how Fibonacci can be effectively combined with other indicators:

- **Moving Averages:** Integrating moving averages with Fibonacci retracement helps confirm trend direction. When Fibonacci levels align with moving average support or resistance, it adds a layer of confirmation to potential entry or exit points.

- **Relative Strength Index (RSI):** RSI is a momentum indicator that can be combined with Fibonacci to identify overbought or oversold conditions. When RSI signals divergence or convergence around Fibonacci levels, it provides additional insight into potential trend reversals.

- **Support and Resistance Zones:** Combining Fibonacci levels with horizontal support and resistance zones strengthens the analysis. Confluence at these zones increases the significance of potential reversal or continuation points, enhancing the reliability of trading signals.

- **Volume Analysis:** Observing trading volume in conjunction with Fibonacci retracement levels provides insights into the strength of a price movement. Volume spikes near Fibonacci levels can confirm the validity of the signal, indicating increased market participation.

- **Chart Patterns:** Recognizing chart patterns, such as triangles, flags, or head and shoulders, alongside Fibonacci levels adds a pattern-based confirmation to technical analysis. Confluence of patterns and Fibonacci retracement levels enhances the likelihood of accurate predictions.

By integrating Fibonacci retracement with complementary indicators, traders create a holistic approach to technical analysis. This comprehensive strategy improves the accuracy of signals and empowers traders to make well-informed decisions in dynamic market conditions.

As we progress through this guide, we will explore practical examples of combining Fibonacci retracement with various indicators, providing you with a nuanced understanding of how to integrate these tools seamlessly in your trading strategy.

CHAPTER 6

PRACTICAL APPLICATIONS OF FIBONACCI RETRACEMENT

6.1 Fibonacci and Support/Resistance Levels

Fibonacci retracement is widely employed in technical analysis to identify and validate support and resistance levels, adding a quantitative dimension to these crucial concepts. Here's a closer look at how Fibonacci enhances the understanding and application of support and resistance:

- **Quantifying Support and Resistance:** Fibonacci retracement levels, particularly the 38.2%, 50%, and 61.8%, serve as dynamic support or resistance zones. When the price approaches these levels, traders assess how the market reacts, providing insights into potential reversals or continuations.

- **Confluence with Horizontal Levels:** Combining Fibonacci levels with traditional horizontal support and resistance levels creates confluence zones. These zones, where multiple levels align, carry increased significance, acting as robust barriers that traders monitor for potential price reactions.

- **Dynamic Support in Uptrends:** In an uptrend, Fibonacci retracement levels act as dynamic support. Traders may look for buying opportunities as the price retraces to these levels, expecting a bounce that confirms the strength of the prevailing upward trend.

- **Dynamic Resistance in Downtrends:** Conversely, in a downtrend, Fibonacci retracement levels act as dynamic resistance. Traders monitor these levels for potential short-selling opportunities, anticipating a reversal as the price retraces upward.

Understanding how Fibonacci retracement interacts with support and resistance levels enables traders to make informed decisions about entry and exit points, as well as to gauge the overall strength of a trend.

6.2 Fibonacci and Trend Reversals

Identifying potential trend reversals is a crucial aspect of trading, and Fibonacci retracement provides a systematic approach to recognizing reversal zones. Here's how

Fibonacci aids in understanding and predicting trend reversals:

- **Spotting Exhaustion Points:** When a trend shows signs of exhaustion, traders often turn to Fibonacci retracement to identify potential reversal points. The 61.8% retracement level, also known as the golden ratio, is particularly significant in this context, indicating a potential shift in market sentiment.

- **Reversal Confirmation with Candlestick Patterns:** Fibonacci levels often align with key candlestick patterns that signal trend reversals, such as doji, engulfing patterns, or hammer patterns. The confluence of Fibonacci levels and candlestick signals strengthens the likelihood of an impending reversal.

- **Divergence Confirmation with Oscillators:** Combining Fibonacci retracement with oscillators like the Relative Strength Index (RSI) or the Moving Average Convergence Divergence (MACD) can provide additional confirmation of trend reversal. Divergence between the oscillator and price at Fibonacci levels may signal an upcoming reversal.

- **Using Fibonacci Time Zones:** Fibonacci time zones, an extension of retracement analysis, can be applied to predict potential reversal dates. Traders observe how price reacts at these time zones, aligning with Fibonacci retracement levels, to confirm or anticipate trend reversals.

The systematic integration of Fibonacci retracement in trend analysis equips traders with a valuable tool for recognizing potential reversals, allowing for timely adjustments to trading strategies.

6.3 Fibonacci and Price Patterns

Fibonacci retracement is often intertwined with various price patterns, enriching the understanding of these patterns and providing additional confirmation for trading decisions. Here's how Fibonacci enhances the interpretation and application of price patterns:

- **Aligning with Harmonic Patterns:** Harmonic patterns, such as the Butterfly, Gartley, or Bat patterns, often incorporate Fibonacci ratios in their structure. Traders apply Fibonacci retracement to confirm the validity of these patterns, providing a quantitative basis for pattern recognition.

- **Enhancing Symmetrical Triangle Analysis:** In symmetrical triangles, Fibonacci retracement assists in identifying potential breakout or breakdown levels. Traders draw Fibonacci retracement lines across the triangle to pinpoint zones where the price is likely to experience a significant move.

- **Validating Head and Shoulders Patterns:** Head and Shoulders patterns, a classic reversal pattern, can be validated with Fibonacci retracement. Traders use retracement levels to assess the depth of the retracement after the completion of the pattern, aiding in setting targets and stop-loss orders.

- **Golden Ratio in Elliott Wave Theory:** Fibonacci retracement levels align closely with Elliott Wave Theory, a popular method for identifying market cycles. The golden ratio often corresponds to the third wave in an Elliott Wave sequence, providing a crucial point for traders to anticipate trend continuation or reversal.

By incorporating Fibonacci retracement into price pattern analysis, traders gain a deeper understanding of the potential price movements associated with these patterns, enhancing the precision of their trading decisions.

6.4 Real-life Trading Examples

To grasp the practical application of Fibonacci retracement, let's examine real-life trading examples across various markets:

- **Example 1: Forex - EUR/USD Uptrend**

In an uptrend, traders identify a swing low at 1.1000 and a swing high at 1.1200. Applying Fibonacci retracement, they observe that the price retraces to the 38.2% level (1.1100) and bounces, confirming the strength of the trend. This becomes an entry point for long positions, with a stop-loss below the 50% level.

- **Example 2: Stocks - Apple Inc.**

Analyzing Apple Inc.'s stock chart, traders identify a strong uptrend. After a significant rally, the price retraces to the 61.8% Fibonacci level. This level coincides with a horizontal support zone. Traders interpret this as a potential reversal area, considering it a buying opportunity with a stop-loss below the Fibonacci level.

- **Example 3: Cryptocurrency - Bitcoin**

During a Bitcoin bull run, traders apply Fibonacci retracement to a price swing. The price retraces to the 50% level, coinciding with a trendline and a key psychological level. Traders see this confluence as a strong support zone, providing a favorable entry point for long positions.

These real-life examples illustrate how Fibonacci retracement is a versatile tool applicable to various asset classes. The systematic use of Fibonacci retracement enhances traders' ability to make informed decisions based on concrete price levels and market dynamics.

As we continue our exploration, we'll delve deeper into advanced applications and case studies, providing you with a comprehensive understanding of how to navigate complex market scenarios using Fibonacci retracement.

CHAPTER 7

PITFALLS AND CHALLENGES IN FIBONACCI ANALYSIS

7.1 Common Mistakes in Using Fibonacci

While Fibonacci retracement is a powerful tool, its application is not without pitfalls. Traders often fall prey to common mistakes that can compromise the effectiveness of their analysis. Recognizing and avoiding these pitfalls is crucial for maximizing the benefits of Fibonacci analysis:

- **Misidentifying Swing Highs and Lows:** One of the primary errors is incorrectly identifying swing highs and lows. Using the wrong points for analysis can lead to inaccurate retracement levels and, consequently, flawed trading decisions.

- **Overlooking Multiple Timeframes:** Traders may focus exclusively on a single timeframe, neglecting the broader market context. Failure to consider multiple timeframes can result in a myopic view, leading to misinterpretation of trends and potential reversal points.

- **Relying Solely on Fibonacci Levels:** While Fibonacci levels are powerful, relying exclusively on them without considering other technical indicators or market factors can be limiting. It's essential to use Fibonacci retracement as part of a comprehensive trading strategy.

- **Ignoring Market Fundamentals:** Traders may become too absorbed in technical analysis and overlook fundamental factors influencing the market. Ignoring economic indicators, news events, or geopolitical developments can lead to missed signals and unexpected market reactions.

7.2 Overcoming Emotional Biases

Emotional biases can significantly impact the application of Fibonacci retracement and cloud judgment. Overcoming these biases is critical for maintaining a disciplined and rational approach to trading:

- **Confirmation Bias:** Traders may seek confirmation of their pre-existing beliefs, leading them to see what they want to see on the charts. It's essential to remain objective and consider alternative scenarios.

- **Fear of Missing Out (FOMO):** The fear of missing out on a potentially profitable trade can lead to impulsive decisions. Establishing clear entry and exit criteria based on Fibonacci levels helps mitigate FOMO-induced trades.

- **Loss Aversion:** The reluctance to accept losses may cause traders to move stop-loss orders or hold losing positions for too long. Adhering to a well-defined risk management plan, including stop-loss orders based on Fibonacci levels, helps counter loss aversion.

- **Overconfidence:** Successful trades based on Fibonacci analysis can breed overconfidence. It's crucial to stay humble and continually reassess market conditions, adapting strategies to evolving situations.

7.3 Adapting to Changing Market Conditions

Market conditions are dynamic, and what works in one environment may not be as effective in another. Adapting Fibonacci analysis to changing market conditions requires flexibility and awareness:

- **Low Volatility Environments:** In periods of low volatility, price movements may not reach significant Fibonacci levels. Traders should adjust expectations and consider using alternative tools or strategies during these market conditions.

- **High Volatility Environments:** High volatility can lead to rapid and unpredictable price movements. Traders may need to widen stop-loss levels or consider shorter timeframes to adapt to the increased market uncertainty.

- **Trendless or Sideways Markets:** In trendless markets, traditional Fibonacci retracement strategies may be less effective. Traders should explore other tools or focus on different aspects of technical analysis, such as chart patterns or momentum indicators.

7.4 Risk Management with Fibonacci

Fibonacci analysis is a valuable component of a comprehensive risk management strategy. Traders can integrate Fibonacci levels into their risk management approach in the following ways:

- **Setting Stop-Loss Orders:** Identifying key Fibonacci retracement levels serves as a foundation for placing stop-loss orders. Traders determine stop-loss levels based on the degree of retracement and their risk tolerance.

- **Position Sizing:** Adjusting the size of positions based on Fibonacci levels and overall market conditions helps manage risk. Traders may opt for smaller positions during uncertain market environments and larger positions when the probability of a trend continuation is higher.

- **Monitoring Risk-Reward Ratios:** Evaluating the risk-reward ratio is a fundamental aspect of risk management. Fibonacci retracement assists traders in setting realistic profit targets and aligning them with potential reversal or continuation zones.

- **Diversification:** Incorporating Fibonacci analysis into a diversified trading strategy reduces reliance on a single tool or approach. Diversification helps spread risk across different trades and mitigates the impact of unsuccessful analyses.

By understanding and addressing these challenges, traders can harness the full potential of Fibonacci retracement in their decision-making process. A disciplined and adaptive approach, combined with a solid risk management framework, enhances the effectiveness of Fibonacci analysis in navigating the complexities of financial markets.

CHAPTER 8

ADVANCED FIBONACCI TECHNIQUES

8.1 Fibonacci Fans

Beyond basic retracement levels, Fibonacci fans are an advanced tool that traders use to identify potential support and resistance zones and trendlines. Here's an in-depth exploration of Fibonacci fans:

- **Concept of Fibonacci Fans:** Fibonacci fans involve drawing trendlines from a significant low or high point and radiating lines at Fibonacci levels, typically 38.2%, 50%, and 61.8%. These diagonal lines create a fan-like structure, providing insights into potential future price movements.

- **Identifying Trendlines:** Fibonacci fans help traders identify trendlines that align with key Fibonacci retracement levels. The intersection of these trendlines with price movements can serve as dynamic support or resistance, offering valuable entry or exit points.

- **Confluence with Horizontal Levels:** Combining Fibonacci fans with horizontal support and resistance levels strengthens the analysis. Confluence zones, where both types of levels intersect, carry increased significance, providing a more robust foundation for trading decisions.

- **Dynamic Trend Analysis:** Fibonacci fans adapt to the evolving trend, making them particularly useful for dynamic trend analysis. As the trend progresses, traders can adjust the placement of Fibonacci fans to capture shifts in market sentiment and identify potential turning points.

8.2 Fibonacci Arcs

Fibonacci arcs introduce a circular element to Fibonacci analysis, offering a unique perspective on potential price movements. Here's a detailed exploration of Fibonacci arcs:

- **Creating Fibonacci Arcs:** To draw Fibonacci arcs, traders select a significant low or high point and place three arcs at Fibonacci levels, typically 38.2%, 50%, and 61.8%. These arcs create curved support and resistance lines that can help predict future price movements.

- **Curve Dynamics:** The curvature of Fibonacci arcs adds a time element to the analysis. As prices move along the arcs, the curves project potential turning points, allowing traders to anticipate reversals or continuations based on the interaction of price with the arcs.

- **Time and Price Alignment:** Fibonacci arcs align time and price, providing a visual representation of how these two dimensions interact. Traders observe where the price intersects with the arcs to identify key reversal or continuation points, enhancing the accuracy of their analysis.

- **Combining with Other Fibonacci Tools:** Fibonacci arcs are often used in conjunction with other Fibonacci tools, such as retracement levels or extensions. This combination of tools enhances the overall precision of the analysis, particularly when multiple Fibonacci elements align.

8.3 Fibonacci Time Zones

Fibonacci time zones extend Fibonacci analysis into the dimension of time, helping traders anticipate potential reversal points based on time cycles. Here's a comprehensive look at Fibonacci time zones:

- **Time-Based Analysis:** Fibonacci time zones involve dividing a significant price movement into specific time intervals based on Fibonacci ratios. These intervals create vertical lines on the chart, indicating potential turning points in the market.

- **Predicting Time-Based Reversals:** Traders use Fibonacci time zones to predict when a trend might experience a reversal or continuation. When the price aligns with a time zone, it suggests a potential inflection point, prompting traders to monitor price action closely for confirmation.

- **Combining with Price Analysis:** To enhance accuracy, Fibonacci time zones are often combined with traditional price analysis tools, such as retracement levels or trendlines. The confluence of time-based and price-based signals strengthens the overall analysis.

- **Adjusting for Market Conditions:** Traders should adapt Fibonacci time zone analysis to current market conditions. In volatile markets, time zones may be compressed, requiring adjustments to the intervals. Conversely, in stable markets, time zones may unfold more gradually.

8.4 Gann and Fibonacci Relationships

The relationship between Gann analysis and Fibonacci retracement adds another layer of complexity to technical analysis. Here's an exploration of how Gann and Fibonacci techniques can be combined:

- **Gann's Square of Nine and Fibonacci Ratios:** Gann's Square of Nine is a tool used in Gann analysis that incorporates Fibonacci ratios. Traders overlay Fibonacci retracement levels on the Square of Nine to identify potential support and resistance zones, aligning with Gann's cyclical theories.

- **Synchronizing Gann Angles with Fibonacci Levels:** Gann angles, representing the balance between time and price, can be synchronized with Fibonacci retracement levels. This alignment enhances the accuracy of trendlines and helps traders identify significant turning points in the market.

- **Time and Price Squares:** Combining Gann and Fibonacci involves analyzing time and price squares. Traders identify key angles and levels within these squares, providing a comprehensive framework for anticipating price movements and potential reversal points.

- **Applying Gann Fan and Fibonacci Fans:** Gann Fan, a tool in Gann analysis, and Fibonacci fans can be applied together. Traders use these fans to identify trendlines and potential support or resistance areas, leveraging the synergy between Gann and Fibonacci principles.

8.5 Fibonacci Confluence Zones

Fibonacci confluence zones occur when multiple Fibonacci elements align at a specific price level, creating a high-probability area for potential reversals or continuations. Here's an in-depth exploration of Fibonacci confluence zones:

- **Definition of Confluence Zones:** Confluence zones occur when two or more Fibonacci elements, such as retracement levels, extensions, arcs, or time zones, align at a specific price point. These zones carry increased significance, often acting as strong support or resistance areas.

- **Enhanced Decision-Making:** Traders prioritize confluence zones as they provide a more robust foundation for decision-making. When multiple Fibonacci elements converge, it increases the likelihood of a price reaction at that level, offering traders clearer entry or exit signals.

- **Combining Different Fibonacci Tools:** Confluence zones result from the combination of various Fibonacci tools. Traders may see alignment between Fibonacci retracement levels, arcs, and time zones, creating a powerful confluence that validates potential market movements.

- **Integration with Other Technical Analysis Tools:** Traders often complement Fibonacci confluence zones with other technical analysis tools, such as trendlines, support/resistance zones, or chart patterns. The convergence of multiple signals increases the reliability of the analysis.

- **Adapting to Changing Market Conditions:** Confluence zones may vary in significance based on market conditions. Traders should adapt their analysis to current volatility, trend strength, and overall market dynamics to accurately interpret the relevance of confluence zones.

Mastering the application of advanced Fibonacci techniques requires practice, an understanding of market dynamics, and the ability to adapt to changing conditions

CHAPTER 9

FIBONACCI IN DIFFERENT TRADING INSTRUMENTS

9.1 Fibonacci in Stocks

Fibonacci retracement is a versatile tool applicable to stock markets, aiding traders in identifying key levels and making informed decisions. Here's a detailed examination of using Fibonacci in stocks:

- **Identifying Trends:** Traders apply Fibonacci retracement to identify trends in stock prices. By anchoring the tool at significant swing highs and lows, they can determine potential retracement levels, helping identify entry and exit points.

- **Support and Resistance:** Fibonacci retracement assists in identifying crucial support and resistance levels in stock charts. These levels often align with key Fibonacci ratios, providing traders with well-defined zones where price reactions are likely.

- **Earnings Reactions:** During earnings seasons, stocks can experience significant price movements. Fibonacci retracement helps traders analyze these moves, identifying potential reversal or continuation points based on the retracement levels.

- **Combining with Fundamental Analysis:** Integrating Fibonacci analysis with fundamental factors enhances decision-making. Traders can align Fibonacci levels with earnings reports, economic indicators, or corporate events to make more comprehensive trading decisions.

9.2 Fibonacci in Forex

Fibonacci analysis is widely employed in the dynamic and fast-paced world of forex trading. Here's how Fibonacci retracement is utilized in the foreign exchange market:

- **Currency Pair Analysis:** Traders in the forex market use Fibonacci retracement to analyze currency pairs. Applying the tool to key price swings helps identify potential reversal or continuation levels, aiding in the formulation of entry and exit strategies.

- **Trend Confirmation:** Fibonacci retracement acts as a tool for confirming trends in the forex market. Traders align the tool with prevailing trends to assess potential retracement levels, offering opportunities to enter trades in the direction of the overall trend.

- **Intraday Trading:** Given the 24-hour nature of the forex market, intraday traders utilize Fibonacci retracement to identify short-term support and resistance levels. This helps them make timely decisions within the context of the broader market trends.

- **Volatility Adjustments:** The forex market can be highly volatile. Fibonacci retracement allows traders to adjust their analysis based on current market conditions, providing insights into potential price movements during periods of both high and low volatility.

9.3 Fibonacci in Cryptocurrency

Cryptocurrency markets, known for their volatility, offer unique challenges and opportunities. Fibonacci retracement is a valuable tool for navigating this landscape:

- **Bitcoin and Altcoins:** Traders use Fibonacci retracement in analyzing both Bitcoin and altcoins. Applying the tool to historical price swings helps identify potential levels where these digital assets may experience reversals or extensions.

- **Speculative Nature:** Cryptocurrencies are often driven by speculation. Fibonacci retracement assists traders in identifying levels where speculative trends might reverse or continue, allowing for well-informed trading decisions.

- **News and Events:** Cryptocurrency markets can be highly reactive to news and events. Fibonacci retracement, when combined with a consideration of fundamental factors, helps traders gauge potential price reactions during significant developments.

- **Long-Term Trend Analysis:** For long-term investors in cryptocurrencies, Fibonacci retracement aids in trend analysis. By identifying key levels based on historical price movements, investors can make informed decisions about when to enter or exit long-term positions.

9.4 Fibonacci in Commodities

Fibonacci retracement is applicable across a range of commodities, from precious metals to energy products. Here's how traders use Fibonacci in commodity markets:

- **Gold and Silver Analysis:** Precious metals like gold and silver exhibit distinct price patterns. Fibonacci retracement assists traders in identifying levels where these metals may experience retracements or extensions, aiding in strategic decision-making.

- **Crude Oil Trends:** Crude oil prices are influenced by various factors. Fibonacci retracement helps traders analyze trends in crude oil, providing insights into potential reversal points or continuation zones based on historical price movements.

- **Agricultural Commodities:** Commodities such as soybeans, wheat, or corn can be subject to seasonal patterns. Fibonacci retracement aids traders in identifying potential retracement or extension levels, taking into account the cyclical nature of agricultural markets.

- **Industrial Metals:** Metals like copper, aluminum, and zinc are influenced by industrial demand. Traders use Fibonacci retracement to analyze price movements in these commodities, identifying key levels where trends might change.

9.5 Fibonacci in Options Trading

Options trading involves unique strategies, and Fibonacci retracement can be integrated into these approaches:

- **Support and Resistance for Options:** Options traders use Fibonacci retracement to identify support and resistance levels. These levels provide insights into potential price movements, aiding in the selection of strike prices and the timing of options trades.

- **Options Expiration Planning:** Fibonacci retracement helps options traders plan for expiration dates. By identifying potential reversal or continuation zones, traders can adjust their options positions or execute new trades based on anticipated price movements.

- **Volatility Considerations:** Options pricing is influenced by volatility. Fibonacci retracement assists options traders in assessing potential price volatility and making decisions about option strategies that align with market conditions.

- **Combining with Implied Volatility:** Traders often combine Fibonacci retracement with implied volatility analysis. This combination allows options traders to gauge potential price movements and select options strategies that align with the expected volatility.

Understanding how Fibonacci retracement applies to different trading instruments empowers traders to make more informed decisions across diverse markets. By adapting Fibonacci techniques to the unique characteristics of each asset class, traders can refine their strategies and navigate the complexities of the financial markets more effectively.

CHAPTER 10

DEVELOPING A FIBONACCI TRADING STRATEGY

10.1 Creating a Systematic Approach

Developing a systematic approach to Fibonacci trading involves establishing a structured framework that guides decision-making. Here's a step-by-step guide to creating a systematic Fibonacci trading strategy:

- **Define Trading Goals:** Clearly articulate your trading goals, whether they are focused on capital preservation, income generation, or capital growth. Establishing specific and measurable objectives provides a foundation for constructing your Fibonacci trading strategy.

- **Select Timeframes:** Choose the timeframes that align with your trading goals and preferences. Fibonacci retracement can be applied across various timeframes, from intraday to long-term. The selected timeframe should match your desired trading style and level of commitment.

- **Identify Trading Instruments:** Determine the financial instruments you'll trade, whether it's stocks, forex, cryptocurrencies, commodities, or a combination. Different asset classes may require adjustments to your Fibonacci strategy based on their unique characteristics.

- **Define Entry and Exit Criteria:** Clearly outline the criteria for entering and exiting trades using Fibonacci retracement. Specify the conditions under which you'll initiate a trade, such as price bouncing off a specific Fibonacci level, and establish clear exit signals based on your goals and risk tolerance.

- **Set Risk-Reward Ratios:** Determine the risk-reward ratios that align with your risk tolerance and trading objectives. Establishing these ratios ensures that your potential profits justify the associated risks and helps guide your position-sizing strategy.

- **Incorporate Additional Indicators:** Consider integrating other technical indicators or tools that complement Fibonacci retracement. This may include moving averages, trendlines, or oscillators. The goal is to create a comprehensive analysis that leverages the strengths of multiple tools.

- **Document Your Strategy:** Record your Fibonacci trading strategy in a detailed document. Include the rules for entering and exiting trades, risk management guidelines, and any additional considerations. Documenting your strategy provides a reference point for consistent decision-making.

10.2 Backtesting Strategies

Backtesting is a crucial step in evaluating the viability and effectiveness of your Fibonacci trading strategy. Here's how to conduct thorough backtesting:

- **Historical Data:** Obtain historical price data for the chosen trading instruments and timeframes. This data should cover a sufficiently long period to capture various market conditions.

- **Simulation Software:** Use trading simulation software or platforms that allow you to apply your Fibonacci strategy to historical data. Simulate trades based on your defined entry and exit criteria, incorporating transaction costs and slippage.

- **Evaluate Performance:** Assess the performance of your strategy by examining key metrics such as profitability, win-loss ratios, and drawdowns. Identify periods of outperformance and underperformance to gain insights into the strategy's strengths and weaknesses.

- **Refinement and Optimization:** Based on the results of your backtesting, refine and optimize your Fibonacci trading strategy. Adjust parameters, fine-tune entry and exit criteria, or consider incorporating additional indicators to improve overall performance.

- **Walk-Forward Testing:** After refining your strategy, conduct walk-forward testing using more recent data to validate its robustness in different market conditions. This step helps ensure that your strategy is adaptive and not overfit to historical data.

10.3 Risk Management and Position Sizing

Effectively managing risk and determining appropriate position sizes are integral components of a successful Fibonacci trading strategy. Here's how to incorporate risk management into your approach:

- **Determine Risk Tolerance:** Clearly define your risk tolerance, which is the maximum amount of capital you are willing to risk on a single trade. This is a crucial parameter in position sizing and helps protect your overall trading capital.

- **Set Stop-Loss Levels:** Utilize Fibonacci retracement levels to set logical stop-loss orders. These levels should align with the strategy's risk-reward ratios and provide a point at which you exit a trade to limit potential losses.

- **Position Sizing Rules:** Establish rules for position sizing based on your risk tolerance and the distance between entry and stop-loss levels. This ensures that the size of each trade is proportionate to the level of risk you are comfortable taking.

- **Diversification:** Consider diversifying your trades across different instruments or asset classes to spread risk. Diversification can help mitigate the impact of adverse price movements in a single position.

- **Regularly Review Risk Management:** Periodically review and adjust your risk management parameters based on changes in market conditions, your risk tolerance, or the overall performance of your Fibonacci trading strategy.

10.4 Adjusting Strategies for Market Conditions

Markets are dynamic, and a successful Fibonacci trading strategy requires adaptability to different conditions. Here's how to adjust your strategy for changing market dynamics:

- **Volatility Assessment:** Regularly assess market volatility and adjust your strategy accordingly. In high-volatility environments, widen stop-loss levels to account for larger price swings. In low-volatility periods, consider tightening stop-loss orders to adapt to smaller price movements.

- **Trend Strength Analysis:** Monitor the strength of market trends and adjust your strategy based on the prevailing conditions. In strong trending markets, consider allowing trades to run for extended periods, while in range-bound markets, focus on shorter-term opportunities.

- **Economic Events and News:** Be mindful of upcoming economic events and news releases that can impact market dynamics. Adjust your trading activity around these events, possibly tightening risk parameters or avoiding trades during periods of heightened uncertainty.

- **Review and Adapt:** Regularly review the performance of your Fibonacci trading strategy and be willing to adapt. If certain elements are consistently underperforming, consider revisiting and refining those aspects to align with current market conditions.

- **Continuous Learning:** Stay informed about market developments, new trading tools, and emerging trends. Continuous learning and staying attuned to market changes allow you to evolve your Fibonacci trading strategy in response to the evolving financial landscape.

Developing and maintaining a successful Fibonacci trading strategy is an ongoing process that requires diligence, adaptability, and a commitment to continuous improvement. By following a systematic approach, conducting thorough backtesting, implementing robust risk management practices, and adjusting strategies to changing market conditions, traders can enhance the effectiveness of their Fibonacci-based trading approach.

CHAPTER 11

INTEGRATING TECHNOLOGY AND AUTOMATION

11.1 Algorithmic Trading with Fibonacci

As technology continues to advance, algorithmic trading has become a prominent feature in financial markets. Integrating Fibonacci analysis into algorithmic trading systems offers numerous advantages:

- **Automated Decision-Making:** Algorithmic trading systems can automatically execute trades based on predefined Fibonacci retracement levels and other criteria. This minimizes the need for manual intervention and ensures swift execution in fast-paced markets.

- **Backtesting and Optimization:** Algorithms allow for efficient backtesting and optimization of Fibonacci-based strategies. Traders can analyze historical data, refine algorithms, and identify optimal parameters, improving the overall performance of the strategy.

- **Real-time Adaptability:** Algorithmic systems can adapt to real-time market conditions, swiftly adjusting to changes in volatility, trends, and other factors. This responsiveness enhances the agility of Fibonacci-based strategies, ensuring they remain effective in dynamic environments.

- **Diversification and Risk Management:** Algorithms can simultaneously manage multiple trades across different instruments and asset classes, incorporating Fibonacci retracement levels for each. This enables effective risk management and diversification, key components of a robust trading strategy.

- **Reduced Emotional Bias:** Algorithmic trading eliminates emotional biases that can influence human decision-making. By adhering strictly to predefined rules, algorithms based on Fibonacci analysis maintain discipline and consistency in trading execution.

11.2 Trading Bots and Fibonacci

Trading bots, or automated trading software, have gained popularity among traders seeking to streamline their operations. Integrating Fibonacci analysis into trading bots can enhance their effectiveness in several ways:

- **24/7 Trading:** Trading bots operate around the clock, leveraging Fibonacci retracement levels to identify potential entry and exit points. This continuous operation allows traders to capture opportunities in different time zones and react promptly to market developments.

- **Instantaneous Execution:** Fibonacci-based trading bots can execute trades almost instantly when predetermined levels are reached. This rapid execution is critical in markets where prices can change rapidly, ensuring that traders capitalize on favorable conditions.

- **Customizable Strategies:** Trading bots can be programmed with customizable Fibonacci-based strategies, allowing traders to fine-tune their approach. Parameters such as retracement levels, risk-reward ratios, and timeframes can be adjusted to align with specific trading preferences.

- **Multi-Exchange Trading:** Trading bots can manage trades across multiple exchanges simultaneously. This capability is particularly valuable in the cryptocurrency market, where assets are listed on various platforms, enabling efficient execution based on Fibonacci analysis.

11.3 Machine Learning and Fibonacci Analysis

Machine learning (ML) has revolutionized the way traders analyze data and make predictions. When integrated with Fibonacci analysis, ML algorithms can adapt and improve over time. Here's how machine learning can enhance Fibonacci-based trading strategies:

- **Pattern Recognition:** ML algorithms excel at pattern recognition, allowing them to identify complex patterns in price movements. When applied to Fibonacci analysis, machine learning can recognize subtle nuances and variations, enhancing the accuracy of retracement level identification.

- **Adaptive Strategies:** ML algorithms can adapt to changing market conditions by continuously learning from new data. This adaptability is particularly beneficial for Fibonacci-based strategies, allowing them to evolve and remain effective in different market environments.

- **Prediction Models:** ML algorithms can be trained to create predictive models based on historical Fibonacci patterns and market data. These models can forecast potential price movements, providing traders with valuable insights for decision-making.

- **Risk Management Optimization:** Machine learning algorithms can optimize risk management parameters by analyzing vast datasets. This can result in more precise stop-loss levels, position sizing, and overall risk-reward ratios within a Fibonacci-based trading strategy.

11.4 The Future of Fibonacci in Trading

The integration of technology and automation in trading, particularly with Fibonacci analysis, is poised to play a pivotal role in the future of financial markets. Here are key trends and possibilities for the future:

- **Enhanced Analytical Tools:** Advanced analytical tools leveraging artificial intelligence (AI) and machine learning will continue to evolve. These tools will offer traders more sophisticated ways to apply Fibonacci analysis, uncover patterns, and make data-driven decisions.

- **Decentralized Finance (DeFi):** As decentralized finance gains prominence, Fibonacci analysis will find applications in the emerging DeFi space. Smart contracts and automated protocols may incorporate Fibonacci-based strategies for decentralized trading and lending.

- **Integration with Quantum Computing:** The advent of quantum computing has the potential to revolutionize complex calculations required in financial markets. Fibonacci-based strategies could benefit from the increased computational power, allowing for more intricate analyses.

- **Blockchain and Cryptocurrencies:** The blockchain technology that underlies cryptocurrencies provides transparent and secure transactional records. Fibonacci-based strategies could integrate seamlessly with blockchain platforms, offering enhanced security and transparency.

- **Collaboration with Traditional Finance:** The blending of traditional and decentralized financial systems may lead to innovative approaches. Fibonacci analysis could play a central role in hybrid financial ecosystems, offering insights for traders across various platforms.

In conclusion, the integration of technology and automation, including algorithmic trading, trading bots, and machine learning, is reshaping the landscape of Fibonacci analysis. As these tools continue to advance, traders can expect more sophisticated and adaptive Fibonacci-based strategies, leading to increased efficiency and effectiveness in navigating the complexities of financial markets.

CHAPTER 12

CASE STUDIES AND SUCCESS STORIES

12.1 Notable Traders Using Fibonacci

Several notable traders have achieved success by incorporating Fibonacci analysis into their trading strategies. These individuals have demonstrated the effectiveness of Fibonacci in navigating financial markets. Here are a few notable traders who have embraced Fibonacci techniques:

- **George Soros:** The legendary investor George Soros is known for using the Fibonacci sequence as part of his broader trading methodology. Soros, famous for his successful currency trades, utilized Fibonacci retracement levels to identify potential reversal points in the foreign exchange market.

- **Paul Tudor Jones:** Renowned hedge fund manager Paul Tudor Jones has publicly acknowledged his use of Fibonacci analysis in his trading decisions. Jones has attributed part of his success to the strategic application of Fibonacci retracement levels in identifying key support and resistance zones.

- **Leonardo Fibonacci (Historical):** The mathematician Leonardo Fibonacci, although not a trader, introduced the Fibonacci sequence to the Western world in the 13th century. His sequence and the golden ratio have since become foundational elements in technical analysis, influencing traders and analysts across generations.

- **Larry Pesavento:** Larry Pesavento is a trader and author who has extensively written about the application of Fibonacci in trading. His work, including the book "Fibonacci Ratios with Pattern Recognition," has contributed to the popularization of Fibonacci analysis in financial markets.

12.2 Case Studies of Successful Trades

Examining specific case studies of successful trades offers insights into how traders leverage Fibonacci analysis to achieve positive outcomes:

- **Trade in an Uptrend:**

- **Scenario:** A stock is in a well-defined uptrend, and a trader identifies a pullback to the 61.8% Fibonacci retracement level.

- **Analysis:** The trader recognizes the 61.8% level as a potential support zone based on Fibonacci analysis.

- **Action:** The trader enters a long position at the Fibonacci level, anticipating a continuation of the uptrend.

- **Result:** The stock bounces off the Fibonacci support, and the trader profits as the uptrend resumes.

- **Reversal Trade Using Fibonacci:**

  - **Scenario:** A currency pair has been in a prolonged downtrend, and a trader observes a potential reversal pattern forming at the 38.2% Fibonacci retracement level.

  - **Analysis:** The trader identifies a bullish reversal pattern (e.g., a double bottom) coinciding with the Fibonacci level.

  - **Action:** Recognizing the confluence of reversal signals, the trader enters a long position, anticipating a trend reversal.

- **Result:** The currency pair reverses direction, and the trader profits from the subsequent uptrend.

- **Cryptocurrency Swing Trade:**

  - **Scenario:** Bitcoin experiences a sharp price correction, and a trader identifies a key Fibonacci retracement level aligning with historical support.

  - **Analysis:** The trader utilizes Fibonacci retracement to identify potential reversal levels in line with historical price patterns.

  - **Action:** The trader enters a long position at the Fibonacci support level, expecting a bounce.

  - **Result:** Bitcoin reverses at the Fibonacci level, and the trader profits from the subsequent upward movement.

12.3 Learning from Failures

While success stories highlight the effectiveness of Fibonacci analysis, learning from failures is equally crucial. Examining instances where Fibonacci analysis did not lead to successful outcomes can provide valuable insights:

- **Overreliance on Fibonacci Alone:**

- **Issue:** A trader solely relies on Fibonacci retracement without considering other technical indicators or market factors.

- **Outcome:** The market reacts unexpectedly to external factors, leading to a failed trade as the trader neglects broader market conditions.

- **Ignoring Fundamentals:**

  - **Issue:** A trader ignores fundamental factors and relies solely on Fibonacci analysis.

  - **Outcome:** Economic news or geopolitical events cause significant market movements that contradict the expected Fibonacci-based outcomes.

- **Failure to Adapt to Changing Conditions:**

  - **Issue:** A trader fails to adapt Fibonacci-based strategies to changing market conditions.

  - **Outcome:** In a highly volatile market, the trader does not adjust risk parameters, leading to increased losses due to unexpected price swings.

Learning from failures involves recognizing the limitations of Fibonacci analysis and understanding that no single tool guarantees success in trading. It emphasizes the importance of a comprehensive approach, combining technical analysis, fundamental factors, and risk management strategies to navigate the complexities of financial markets effectively.

In conclusion, case studies of successful trades and learning from failures demonstrate the dynamic nature of Fibonacci analysis in trading. Notable traders and historical figures have successfully employed Fibonacci techniques, highlighting its enduring relevance in the world of finance. Analyzing specific cases provides valuable insights for traders looking to integrate Fibonacci into their own strategies while emphasizing the importance of a well-rounded approach to trading.

CHAPTER 13

MASTERING FIBONACCI PSYCHOLOGY

13.1 Building Confidence in Fibonacci Analysis

Building confidence in Fibonacci analysis is a crucial aspect of mastering its application in trading. Here are key steps to foster confidence:

- **Education and Understanding:** Thoroughly educate yourself about Fibonacci analysis, including retracement levels, extensions, and additional tools. Understand the underlying mathematical principles and how they are applied in financial markets.

- **Backtesting Success:** Conduct extensive backtesting of Fibonacci-based strategies using historical data. Successful backtesting results can instill confidence in the effectiveness of Fibonacci analysis and provide a foundation for real-world application.

- **Start with Simulated Trading:** Begin by applying Fibonacci analysis in a simulated or demo trading environment. This allows you to practice without risking real capital, gaining hands-on experience and building confidence in your ability to interpret Fibonacci signals.

- **Review Success Stories:** Study success stories and case studies of traders who have effectively used Fibonacci analysis. Analyzing real-world examples can enhance your understanding and confidence in the practical application of Fibonacci techniques.

- **Incremental Real Trades:** Gradually transition to real trades with small positions as you gain confidence. Starting with smaller trades allows you to validate your analysis in live markets while managing risk effectively.

- **Continuous Learning:** Stay informed about developments in Fibonacci analysis and related tools. Continuous learning and staying updated on market dynamics contribute to a deeper understanding, reinforcing your confidence in applying Fibonacci techniques.

13.2 Overcoming Trading Anxiety

Trading anxiety can hinder effective decision-making. Overcoming anxiety when using Fibonacci analysis involves addressing psychological factors:

- **Acceptance of Uncertainty:** Acknowledge that uncertainty is inherent in financial markets. While Fibonacci analysis provides valuable insights, no strategy guarantees success. Embrace uncertainty as a natural part of trading.

- **Risk Management Strategies:** Implement robust risk management strategies that align with your risk tolerance. Knowing that you have predefined risk limits can help alleviate anxiety by providing a clear framework for decision-making.

- **Visualization Techniques:** Use visualization techniques to mentally prepare for different market scenarios. Visualizing successful trades based on Fibonacci analysis can help build confidence and reduce anxiety.

- **Mindfulness and Focus:** Practice mindfulness to stay present and focused during trading. Anxiety often stems from dwelling on past losses or worrying about future outcomes. Staying in the present moment allows for more objective decision-making.

- **Regular Breaks:** Take regular breaks to prevent burnout and reduce stress. Trading continuously without breaks can contribute to anxiety. Step away from the screen periodically to refresh your mind.

- **Seek Support:** Connect with fellow traders or mentors to share experiences and insights. Discussing challenges and successes with others can provide a support system and help alleviate anxiety.

13.3 Patience and Discipline in Fibonacci Trading

Patience and discipline are foundational elements in successful Fibonacci trading. Here's how to cultivate and maintain these qualities:

- **Define Clear Trading Plans:** Develop clear and well-defined trading plans that incorporate Fibonacci analysis. Knowing your entry and exit points, as well as risk management strategies, enhances discipline and reduces impulsive decisions.

- **Wait for Confirmation:** Exercise patience by waiting for confirmation of Fibonacci signals. Avoid entering trades based on preliminary signals alone. Wait for price action to confirm the validity of the identified Fibonacci levels.

- **Stick to Your Strategy:** Discipline involves sticking to your predefined strategy, even when faced with market fluctuations. Trust in your analysis and resist the temptation to deviate from your plan in response to short-term market movements.

- **Journaling and Review:** Maintain a trading journal to track your decisions and outcomes. Regularly review your journal to identify areas where discipline may have lapsed. Reflecting on past trades fosters self-awareness and reinforces the importance of discipline.

- **Set Realistic Expectations:** Establish realistic expectations regarding the frequency of trading opportunities. Not every market condition is conducive to Fibonacci-based trades. Patience involves waiting for high-probability setups and not forcing trades in unfavorable conditions.

- **Mindful Decision-Making:** Practice mindfulness during trading to remain focused on the present moment. Mindful decision-making reduces impulsivity and fosters a disciplined approach to following your trading plan.

13.4 Developing a Winning Mindset

A winning mindset is crucial for success in Fibonacci trading. Cultivate a mindset that promotes resilience, adaptability, and continuous improvement:

- **Positive Self-Talk:** Monitor your internal dialogue and replace negative thoughts with positive affirmations. Positive self-talk contributes to a more optimistic and resilient mindset, helping you navigate challenges with confidence.

- **Learning from Setbacks:** View setbacks as opportunities for learning and improvement rather than failures. Analyze losing trades objectively, identify areas for improvement, and apply those lessons in future trading endeavors.

- **Adaptability:** Embrace adaptability as markets evolve. A winning mindset involves being open to adjusting your strategies based on changing market conditions, continuously refining your approach to stay ahead.

- **Focus on Process, Not Just Outcomes:** Shift your focus from purely outcome-based thinking to a process-oriented mindset. Concentrate on executing your trading plan effectively, making disciplined decisions, and applying sound risk management, recognizing that positive outcomes will follow.

- **Celebrate Small Wins:** Acknowledge and celebrate small wins along the way. Recognizing your achievements, even if they are incremental, fosters a positive mindset and reinforces the idea that success is a continuous journey.

- **Continuous Learning:** Cultivate a mindset of continuous learning. Stay curious about market trends, new tools, and evolving trading strategies. A mindset of continuous improvement positions you for long-term success in Fibonacci trading.

Mastering Fibonacci psychology involves not only understanding the technical aspects of analysis but also developing the mental resilience and discipline required for successful trading. By building confidence, overcoming anxiety, practicing patience and discipline, and fostering a winning mindset, traders can enhance their ability to effectively apply Fibonacci analysis and navigate the complexities of financial markets.

CHAPTER 14

CONTINUOUS LEARNING AND IMPROVEMENT

14.1 Staying Updated on Market Trends

Staying updated on market trends is a cornerstone of continuous learning for traders using Fibonacci analysis. Here's how to remain informed and adapt to changing market dynamics:

- **Market Research:** Regularly conduct market research to stay informed about global economic trends, geopolitical events, and changes in market sentiment. Understanding the broader market context enhances your ability to apply Fibonacci analysis effectively.

- **News and Information Sources:** Utilize reputable news sources, financial publications, and market analysis reports to stay abreast of current events. Real-time information enables you to make timely decisions and adjust your Fibonacci-based strategies as needed.

- **Economic Calendars:** Monitor economic calendars for scheduled releases of economic indicators, central bank announcements, and other events that can impact financial markets. These events may influence Fibonacci retracement levels and require adjustments to your trading approach.

- **Technical Analysis Updates:** Stay updated on advancements in technical analysis, including tools and indicators that complement Fibonacci analysis. Incorporating new techniques can enhance the accuracy and effectiveness of your trading strategies.

14.2 Evolving with Technology

Technological advancements play a crucial role in the evolution of trading strategies. Traders utilizing Fibonacci analysis should embrace and adapt to technological changes:

- **Advanced Analytical Tools:** Explore and integrate advanced analytical tools that leverage artificial intelligence (AI), machine learning, and big data analytics. These tools can enhance the precision of

Fibonacci analysis and provide deeper insights into market patterns.

- **Algorithmic Trading Platforms:** Familiarize yourself with algorithmic trading platforms that enable automated execution of Fibonacci-based strategies. Algorithmic trading enhances efficiency and allows for real-time adaptation to changing market conditions.

- **Mobile Trading Apps:** Utilize mobile trading apps that offer flexibility and accessibility. Mobile apps enable you to monitor markets, execute trades, and manage your Fibonacci-based strategies on the go, ensuring you stay connected to the markets at all times.

- **Blockchain and Decentralized Finance (DeFi):** Stay informed about developments in blockchain technology and the emergence of decentralized finance. The integration of Fibonacci analysis with blockchain platforms may present new opportunities for traders in the evolving financial landscape.

14.3 Networking and Learning from Peers

Engaging with a community of peers is a valuable strategy for continuous learning and improvement. Here's how networking can contribute to your growth as a trader:

- **Online Forums and Communities:** Join online forums and communities where traders share insights, experiences, and strategies. Participating in discussions exposes you to diverse perspectives and allows you to learn from the successes and challenges of others.

- **Social Media Platforms:** Follow reputable traders, analysts, and financial institutions on social media platforms. These platforms provide real-time updates, market commentary, and educational content that can contribute to your understanding of Fibonacci analysis.

- **Networking Events and Conferences:** Attend trading conferences, seminars, and networking events. Connecting with industry professionals and experienced traders offers opportunities for mentorship, knowledge exchange, and exposure to different trading styles.

- **Collaborative Learning:** Form study groups or trading circles with peers who share an interest in Fibonacci analysis. Collaborative learning environments provide a space for discussing strategies, reviewing trades, and collectively enhancing your understanding of market dynamics.

14.4 Embracing Lifelong Learning

The commitment to lifelong learning is fundamental for traders seeking sustained success. Here's how to embrace a mindset of continuous improvement:

- **Reading and Education:** Continuously read books, articles, and research papers on trading, technical analysis, and financial markets. Formal education, such as courses and workshops, can deepen your understanding of Fibonacci analysis and related topics.

- **Reflecting on Trades:** Regularly review your trades and outcomes, whether successful or unsuccessful. Reflecting on your decisions fosters self-awareness, identifies areas for improvement, and contributes to a continuous learning cycle.

- **Seeking Feedback:** Seek feedback from mentors, peers, or trading communities. Constructive feedback provides valuable insights into blind spots, behavioral patterns, and potential refinements to your Fibonacci-based strategies.

- **Adaptability and Open-mindedness:** Cultivate an adaptable and open-minded approach to learning. Markets evolve, and embracing new ideas, tools, and techniques ensures that your Fibonacci analysis remains relevant and effective in different market conditions.

- **Journaling:** Maintain a trading journal to document your thoughts, decisions, and emotions during each trade. Journaling provides a tangible record of your journey, serving as a reference for self-assessment and ongoing improvement.

In conclusion, continuous learning and improvement are integral to success in trading with Fibonacci analysis. Staying updated on market trends, embracing technological advancements, networking with peers, and maintaining a mindset of lifelong learning contribute to a trader's ability to navigate the complexities of financial markets effectively. By evolving with the ever-changing landscape of trading, traders using Fibonacci analysis position themselves for long-term success and adaptability in dynamic market conditions.

CHAPTER 15

THE FUTURE OF FIBONACCI IN FINANCIAL MARKETS

15.1 Emerging Trends in Technical Analysis

As financial markets evolve, new trends in technical analysis are likely to shape the future landscape. Traders using Fibonacci analysis should stay attuned to these emerging trends:

- **Artificial Intelligence (AI) Integration:** The integration of AI into technical analysis tools is expected to enhance pattern recognition and predictive modeling. Fibonacci analysis, combined with AI algorithms, may lead to more accurate and adaptive trading strategies.

- **Quantum Computing:** The potential use of quantum computing in financial markets could revolutionize complex calculations required for advanced Fibonacci analysis. Quantum computing may enable traders to process vast datasets and perform intricate analyses in real-time.

- **Machine Learning Enhancements:** Continuous advancements in machine learning techniques will likely lead to more sophisticated models for Fibonacci analysis. Machine learning algorithms may adapt more effectively to changing market conditions and identify subtle patterns in price movements.

- **Decentralized Finance (DeFi):** The rise of decentralized finance presents opportunities for Fibonacci analysis to be integrated into smart contracts and decentralized trading platforms. DeFi could reshape the way traders apply Fibonacci strategies in a more decentralized and transparent financial ecosystem.

15.2 Potential Developments in Fibonacci Analysis

The future of Fibonacci analysis holds the promise of several potential developments that could enhance its application in financial markets:

- **Dynamic Fibonacci Levels:** Developments in technology may lead to the creation of dynamic Fibonacci levels that adapt to changing market conditions. These dynamic levels could provide more accurate and responsive signals for traders.

- **Automated Pattern Recognition:** Advanced algorithms may automate the recognition of Fibonacci patterns, streamlining the analysis process for traders. Automated pattern recognition could identify complex Fibonacci formations more efficiently than traditional manual methods.

- **Integration with Fundamental Analysis:** Future developments may involve the seamless integration of Fibonacci analysis with fundamental analysis. Combining technical and fundamental factors could offer a more comprehensive approach to decision-making for traders.

- **Enhanced Visualization Tools:** Improved visualization tools may provide traders with more intuitive and user-friendly interfaces for applying Fibonacci analysis. Enhanced visualization can simplify the interpretation of Fibonacci patterns and levels.

15.3 Adapting to Regulatory Changes

As regulatory environments in financial markets evolve, traders using Fibonacci analysis must adapt to changes in compliance and governance. Key considerations include:

- **Regulatory Scrutiny:** Increased scrutiny from regulatory bodies may lead to more transparent reporting and disclosure requirements for traders. Understanding and complying with regulatory changes is essential to maintaining the integrity of Fibonacci-based trading strategies.

- **Privacy and Data Security:** Heightened concerns about privacy and data security may result in stricter regulations regarding the handling of financial data. Traders must stay informed about data protection requirements and implement robust security measures.

- **Leverage and Risk Management:** Regulatory changes may impact leverage limits and risk management practices. Traders using Fibonacci analysis should be prepared to adjust their strategies and position sizes to align with evolving regulatory standards.

15.4 Sustainability and Ethical Trading

The future of financial markets is likely to witness a growing emphasis on sustainability and ethical trading practices. Traders using Fibonacci analysis can align with these trends by:

- **Environmental, Social, and Governance (ESG) Integration:** Incorporating ESG factors into trading strategies alongside Fibonacci analysis may become more prevalent. Traders may consider the environmental and social impact of their trades and investments.

- **Impact Investing:** The integration of Fibonacci analysis with impact investing principles may gain traction. Traders could align their strategies with companies and assets that demonstrate positive societal and environmental impacts.

- **Ethical Algorithmic Trading:** The development of ethical guidelines for algorithmic trading, including Fibonacci-based algorithms, may be on the horizon. Adhering to ethical principles in algorithmic trading ensures responsible and socially conscious market participation.

- **Transparency in Trading Practices:** Future trading practices may prioritize transparency, requiring traders to disclose their methodologies, including the use of Fibonacci analysis. Transparency fosters trust and aligns with the growing demand for ethical trading behavior.

In conclusion, the future of Fibonacci in financial markets holds exciting possibilities and challenges. Traders can position themselves for success by embracing emerging trends in technical analysis, anticipating potential developments in Fibonacci analysis, adapting to regulatory changes, and incorporating sustainability and ethical considerations into their trading strategies. By staying informed and remaining flexible in the face of evolving market dynamics, traders using Fibonacci analysis can navigate the future landscape of financial markets with confidence and resilience.

APPENDIX

FIBONACCI RESOURCES AND TOOLS

Recommended Books:

1. **"Fibonacci Ratios with Pattern Recognition" by Larry Pesavento:** A comprehensive guide by an experienced trader, offering insights into Fibonacci ratios and their application in pattern recognition for trading.

2. **"Fibonacci Trading: How to Master the Time and Price Advantage" by Carolyn Boroden:** This book provides a detailed exploration of Fibonacci time and price analysis, offering practical strategies for traders.

3. **"The Complete Guide to Fibonacci Trading and Phi Phenomenon" by George M. Protonotarios:** An in-

depth resource covering both the theory and practical applications of Fibonacci trading, with a focus on the Phi phenomenon.

4. **"Fibonacci Applications and Strategies for Traders" by Robert Fischer and Jens Fischer:** This book delves into various Fibonacci trading strategies, providing real-world examples and applications for traders.

5. **"The Mathematics of Financial Modeling and Investment Management" by Sergio M. Focardi and Frank J. Fabozzi:** While not solely focused on Fibonacci, this book explores mathematical concepts essential for understanding quantitative aspects of trading, including Fibonacci analysis.

Online Courses:

1. **Investopedia Academy - Fibonacci Retracement and Extension:** This online course covers the fundamentals of Fibonacci retracement and extension, guiding learners through practical applications in trading.

2. **Udemy - Fibonacci Trading: Learn How to Trade with Fibonacci:** A beginner-friendly course that introduces learners to the basics of Fibonacci trading, including retracement levels, extensions, and practical trading strategies.

3. **Coursera - Technical Analysis and the Fibonacci Ratio:** Offered by reputable institutions, this course provides a broader perspective on technical analysis, with a focus on the Fibonacci ratio and its applications.

Trading Software and Tools:

1. **MetaTrader 4 (MT4) and MetaTrader 5 (MT5):** Widely used trading platforms that include Fibonacci retracement tools. Traders can draw Fibonacci levels directly on price charts.

2. **TradingView:** A popular charting platform that integrates Fibonacci retracement and extension tools, providing a user-friendly interface for technical analysis.

3. **Thinkorswim:** A trading platform by TD Ameritrade that offers advanced charting tools, including Fibonacci retracement and extension drawing capabilities.

4. **Fibonacci Calculator:** Online calculators are available for quickly determining Fibonacci retracement and extension levels based on price data.

Glossary:

1. **Fibonacci Retracement:** A technical analysis tool that identifies potential levels of support or resistance

based on the Fibonacci sequence, commonly used to predict price reversals.

2. **Fibonacci Extension:** An extension of the Fibonacci retracement, indicating potential levels where the price might extend beyond the original trend.

3. **Golden Ratio:** A mathematical concept represented by the number Phi (approximately 1.618), often used in Fibonacci analysis to identify key retracement levels.

4. **Fibonacci Sequence:** A series of numbers where each number is the sum of the two preceding ones, starting with 0 and 1 (0, 1, 1, 2, 3, 5, 8, 13, ...).

5. **Bullish Trend:** A market trend characterized by rising prices over time, indicating an upward movement.

6. **Bearish Trend:** A market trend characterized by falling prices over time, indicating a downward movement.

7. **Confluence:** The occurrence of multiple technical analysis factors, such as Fibonacci levels, aligning at the same price point, increasing their significance.

8. **Algorithmic Trading:** The use of computer algorithms to execute trades automatically based on predefined criteria, including Fibonacci analysis.

Key Terms and Concepts:

1. **Fibonacci Fans:** Lines drawn on a price chart to identify potential areas of support or resistance based on Fibonacci retracement levels.

2. **Fibonacci Arcs:** Curved lines drawn on a price chart to identify potential areas of future support or resistance based on Fibonacci retracement levels.

3. **Fibonacci Time Zones:** A tool used to identify potential reversal points based on Fibonacci time ratios rather than price levels.

4. **Gann and Fibonacci Relationships:** The exploration of potential connections between Gann analysis and Fibonacci analysis in predicting market movements.

5. **Fibonacci Confluence Zones:** Areas where multiple Fibonacci retracement or extension levels coincide, adding strength to their significance as potential support or resistance levels.